Robert Munsch

by Chelsea Donaldson

Gail Saunders-Smith, PhD, Consulting Editor

CAPSTONE PRESS
a capstone imprint

Pebble Plus is published by Capstone Press,
1710 Roe Crest Drive, North Mankato, Minnesota 56003
www.capstonepub.com

Cataloging-in-publication data is on file with the Library of Congress.
ISBN 978-1-4914-1960-1 (library binding)
ISBN 978-1-4914-1979-3 (paperback)
ISBN 978-1-4914-1992-2 (eBook PDF)
Written by Chelsea Donaldson

Developed and Produced by Focus Strategic Communications, Inc.
Adrianna Edwards: project manager
Ron Edwards: editor
Rob Scanlan: designer and compositor
Karen Hunter: media researcher

Photo Credits
Annick Press: title page, "Mortimer" © Robert Munsch, 1983 (text), Michael Martchen (art), 9, "Mud Puddles" © Robert Munsch, 1979 (text), Sami Suomalainen (art), 13, "David's Father" © Robert Munsch, 1983 (text), Michael Martchen (art), 15, "I Have To Go" © Robert Munsch, 1986 (text), Michael Martchen (art), 15, "The Paperbag Princess", "PIGS" © Robert Munsch, 1992 (text), Michael Martchen (art), 15, "Something Good" © Robert Munsch, 1995 (text), Michael Martchen (art), 15; published by Annick Press Ltd. All rights reserved. Reproduced by permission; Associated Press: 11 the Canadian Press/Frank Gunn; Getty Images: WireImage/Getty Images, 19; Robert Munsch: 5, 17, 21; Wikipedia, 7.

Note to Parents and Teachers
The Canadian Biographies set supports national curriculum standards for social studies related to people and culture. This book describes and illustrates Robert Munsch. The images support early readers in understanding text. The repetition of words and phrases helps early readers learn new words. This book also introduces early readers to subject-specific vocabulary words, which are defined in the Glossary section. Early readers may need assistance to read some words and to use the Table of Contents, Glossary, Read More, Internet Sites, and Index sections of the book.

Printed in China by Leo Paper Group in 2014
007039LEOF14

Table of Contents

Early Years

Famous children's book author
Robert Munsch was born in 1945.
He was one of nine kids
in his family. They lived
in Pittsburgh, Pennsylvania.

born in
Pittsburgh,
Pennsylvania

1945

Robert as a young boy

Robert didn't like school much.

He often wrote poetry

to pass time. After high school

Robert studied to be a priest.

Seven years later he left school.

He started working at a day care.

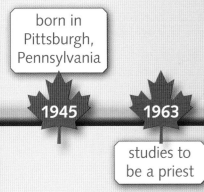

born in
Pittsburgh,
Pennsylvania

1945

1963

studies to
be a priest

Robert studied to be a priest at Fordham University.

Finding His Way

Robert liked telling the day care children silly stories. His first story was called "Mortimer." It is about a boy who would rather sing than sleep.

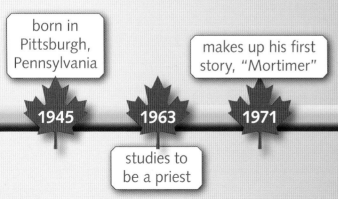

born in Pittsburgh, Pennsylvania

1945

studies to be a priest

1963

makes up his first story, "Mortimer"

1971

MORTIMER

STORY • ROBERT MUNSCH
ART • MICHAEL MARTCHENKO

CLASSIC MUNSCH

Mortimer wasn't an actual book until 1983.

At the day care Robert met Ann Beeler. In 1973 Robert and Ann married. Two years later they moved to Canada. They both worked at a day care there.

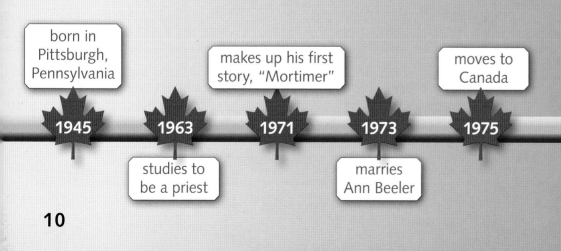

born in Pittsburgh, Pennsylvania

makes up his first story, "Mortimer"

moves to Canada

1945   1963   1971   1973   1975

studies to be a priest

marries Ann Beeler

Children reading Robert's books at a day care

Becoming an Author

One day Robert made up
a story about a mud puddle.
In the story a puddle jumped
from a tree. In 1979 *Mud Puddle*
became Robert's first book.

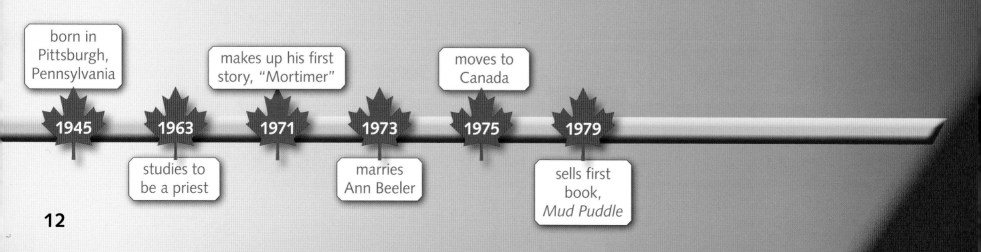

born in
Pittsburgh,
Pennsylvania

makes up his first
story, "Mortimer"

moves to
Canada

1945   **1963**   **1971**   **1973**   **1975**   **1979**

studies to
be a priest

marries
Ann Beeler

sells first
book,
Mud Puddle

Mud Puddle

Story Robert Munsch
Art Sami Suomalainen

CLASSIC MUNSCH

Robert's first book, *Mud Puddle*

Since then Robert has written
more than 50 books.
He enjoys visiting schools.
Sometimes he writes stories
about children he meets.

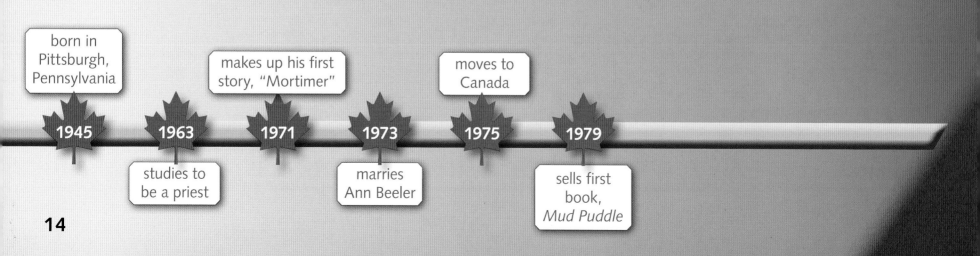

born in
Pittsburgh,
Pennsylvania

makes up his first
story, "Mortimer"

moves to
Canada

1945

1963

1971

1973

1975

1979

studies to
be a priest

marries
Ann Beeler

sells first
book,
Mud Puddle

DAVID'S FATHER

STORY · ROBERT MUNSCH   ART · MICHAEL MARTCHENKO

I HAVE TO GO!

Story by Robert Munsch
Art by Michael Martchenko

The Paper Bag Princess

Story · Robert Munsch   Art · Michael Martchenko

PIGS

by Robert Munsch   art by Michael Martchenko

SOMETHING GOOD

by Robert Munsch
art by Michael Martchenko

Some of Robert's books

15

His most popular book is *Love You Forever*. It is about a mother's love for her children. It sold more copies than any other Canadian children's book.

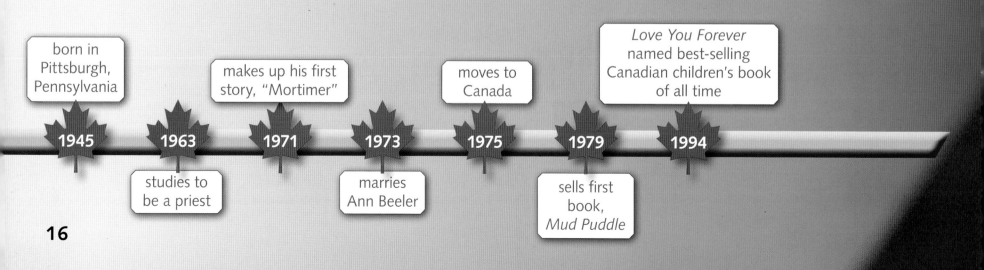

born in Pittsburgh, Pennsylvania

makes up his first story, "Mortimer"

moves to Canada

Love You Forever named best-selling Canadian children's book of all time

1945　1963　1971　1973　1975　1979　1994

studies to be a priest

marries Ann Beeler

sells first book, *Mud Puddle*

Robert in 1996

In 1999 Robert was given

the Order of Canada.

The award is given to Canadians

who improve their country.

Few people receive the award.

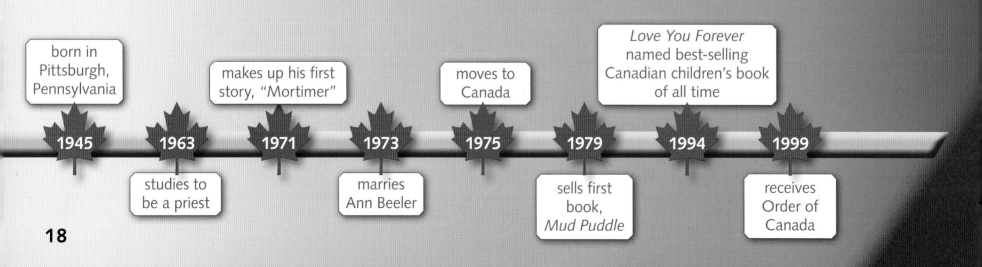

born in
Pittsburgh,
Pennsylvania

makes up his first
story, "Mortimer"

moves to
Canada

Love You Forever
named best-selling
Canadian children's book
of all time

1945   1963   1971   1973   1975   1979   1994   1999

studies to
be a priest

marries
Ann Beeler

sells first
book,
Mud Puddle

receives
Order of
Canada

In 2009 Robert also got his name on the Walk of Fame.

Challenges

In 2008 Robert had a stroke. Afterwards he had a hard time speaking. But now he can tell stories again. Robert's books still charm children all around the world.

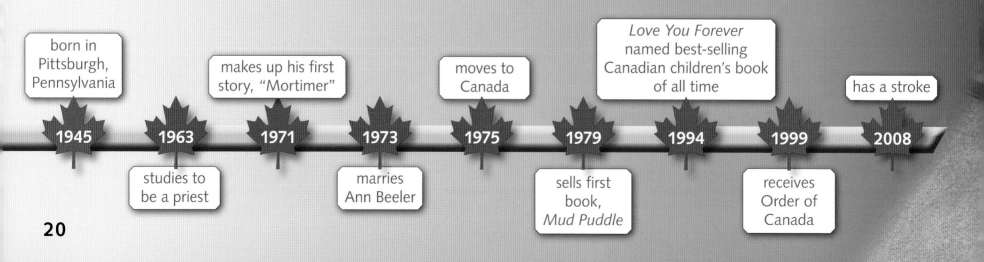

born in Pittsburgh, Pennsylvania

makes up his first story, "Mortimer"

moves to Canada

Love You Forever named best-selling Canadian children's book of all time

has a stroke

1945   **1963**   **1971**   **1973**   **1975**   **1979**   **1994**   **1999**   **2008**

studies to be a priest

marries Ann Beeler

sells first book, *Mud Puddle*

receives Order of Canada

Robert visiting kids in a school library

21

Glossary

author—a person who writes books

improve—to make something better

Order of Canada—an award given to Canadians who do something special to make the country a better place

priest—a minister in the Catholic church

stroke—a brain illness that can affect how a person speaks or moves

Read More

Kissock, Heather. *Robert Munsch. Remarkable Writers.* Calgary: Weigl, 2012.

Internet Sites

FactHound offers a safe, fun way to find Internet sites related to this book. All of the sites on FactHound have been researched by our staff.

Here's all you do:

Visit *www.facthound.com*

Type in this code: 9781491419601

 Check out projects, games and lots more at **www.capstonekids.com**

Index

Word Count: 238
Grade: 1
Early-Intervention Level: 15